INSIDE THE NFL

SEATTLE SEAHAWKS

by Ted Coleman

Abdo & Daughters
MIDDLE GRADE NONFICTION

An imprint of Abdo Publishing
abdobooks.com

ABDOBOOKS.COM

Published by Abdo Publishing, a division of ABDO, PO Box 398166, Minneapolis, Minnesota 55439.

Printed in China.
052025
092025

THIS BOOK CONTAINS RECYCLED MATERIALS

Cover Photos: Cooper Neill/Getty Images Sport/Getty Images (D. K. Metcalf); Focus on Sport/Getty Images Sport/Getty Images (Steve Largent)
Interior Photos: Christian Petersen/Getty Images Sport/Getty Images, 4–5, 6, 61 (top right); Otto Greule Jr./Getty Images Sport/Getty Images, 7, 38, 50, 53; Tom Pennington/Getty Images Sport/Getty Images, 8; Kevin C. Cox/Getty Images Sport/Getty Images, 9; Abdo Publishing, 10–11, 58; Charles E. Rotkin/VCG/Corbis Historical/Getty Images, 12–13; Michael Zagaris/Getty Images Sport/Getty Images, 14–15, 52, 60 (bottom left); Peter Read Miller/AP Images, 16; Rick Stewart/Getty Images Sport/Getty Images, 17; Al Messerschmidt Archive/AP Images, 18, 19; Focus on Sport/Getty Images, 20–21; Kirby Lee/Getty Images Sport/Getty Images, 22; Barry Sweet/AP Images, 23 (top); Cheryl Hatch/AP Images, 23 (bottom); Bill Haber/AP Images, 24–25; John Hayes/AP Images, 26; Stephen Brashear/Getty Images Sport/Getty Images, 28 (top), 43; John Froschauer/AP Images, 28 (bottom); George Gojkovich/Getty Images Sport/Getty Images, 29; Greg Trott/AP Images, 30; Jonathan Daniel/Getty Images Sport/Getty Images, 31; John Medina/Getty Images Sport/Getty Images, 32, 60 (bottom right); Miles Kennedy/AP Images, 33; Elise Amendola/AP Images, 35, 60 (top); Ted S. Warren/AP Images, 36–37, 61 (top left); Jonathan Ferrey/Getty Images Sport/Getty Images, 39; Thearon W. Henderson/Getty Images Sport/Getty Images, 40; Dilip Vishwanat/Getty Images Sport/ Getty Images, 41; Ronald Martinez/Getty Images Sport/Getty Images, 44, 63; Paul Kitagaki Jr./The Sacramento Bee/AP Images, 45; Rich Kane/Icon Sports Media/Corbis/Icon Sportswire/Getty Images, 46; Matt Slocum/AP Images, 47, 61 (bottom left); Elsa/Getty Images Sport/Getty Images, 48–49; David J. Phillip/AP Images, 51; Hannah Foslien/Getty Images Sport/Getty Images, 54; Kevin Terrell/AP Images, 55; Andy Lewis/Icon Sportswire/Getty Images, 56; Steph Chambers/Getty Images Sport/Getty Images, 57; Jane Gershovich/Getty Images Sport/Getty Images, 59, 61 (bottom right)

Editor: Haley Williams
Series Designer: Laura Graphenteen
Production Designer: Ebonee Estrella

Library of Congress Control Number: 2024948469

Publisher's Cataloging-in-Publication Data

Names: Coleman, Ted, author.
Title: Seattle Seahawks / by Ted Coleman
Description: Minneapolis, Minnesota: Abdo Publishing, 2026 | Series: Inside the NFL | Includes online resources and index.
Identifiers: ISBN 9781098296902 (lib. bdg.) | ISBN 9798384919421 (ebook)
Subjects: LCSH: Seattle Seahawks (Football team)--Juvenile literature. | National Football League--Juvenile literature. | Football teams--Juvenile literature. | American football--Juvenile literature.
Classification: DDC 796.333--dc23

CONTENTS

Seattle Seahawks quarterback Russell Wilson goes to pass in the NFC Championship Game against the Green Bay Packers in January 2015.

CHAPTER 1

AN IMPROBABLE COMEBACK

The Seattle Seahawks needed a big play. Overtime had just begun in the National Football Conference (NFC) Championship Game in January 2015. But four plays in, Seattle faced third-and-seven from their own 30-yard line. With the game against the Green Bay Packers on the line, Seattle quarterback Russell Wilson took the snap and dropped back to pass. Wilson uncorked one of his best passes of the day right into the hands of wide receiver Doug Baldwin for a 35-yard gain.

The remaining 35 yards to the end zone, along with the Packers' defense, was all that stood between Seattle and a second consecutive appearance in the Super Bowl. But the fact that the Seahawks were even playing in overtime was a feat in itself. At halftime, it had seemed as though Seattle didn't have a chance of winning.

Running back Marshawn Lynch (24) ran for 157 yards in the NFC title game.

GETTING TRICKY

In the third quarter of the NFC title game, the Seahawks lined up to attempt a field goal. As holder Jon Ryan caught the snap, kicker Stephen Hauschka appeared as though he would kick the ball. But at the last second, Ryan pulled the ball away. The Seahawks had faked the field goal. Ryan scurried to his left and keyed in on offensive tackle Garry Gilliam, who was wide-open down the field. Ryan delivered a 19-yard pass to Gilliam for a touchdown to give Seattle its first score of the game.

NOT BACKING DOWN

Seattle came into the game as defending Super Bowl champions. But in the first half against the Packers, Wilson threw three interceptions, and the team didn't score. The typically loud Seattle crowd grew quiet. Wilson, however, never gave up hope. "Hey, you know the score is only 16–0," he told his teammates.

The Seahawks cut into the lead in the third quarter with a touchdown. The score was 19–7 when Seattle took over at its own 31-yard line with 3:52 left to play. On the next play, the Seahawks' powerful running back Marshawn Lynch charged forward for a 14-yard gain. Then Wilson completed 20- and 26-yard passes to move the team farther down the field. Within about 90 seconds, the Seahawks reached the Green Bay 1-yard line.

One of the things that made Wilson a special quarterback was his ability to run as well as pass. And on third down from the 1-yard line, Wilson took the snap, then quickly cut to his left away from a Packers defender. That defender grabbed nothing but air as Wilson jogged into the end zone to make the score 19–14.

Wilson runs past a Green Bay defender for a touchdown.

After recovering an onside kick, Seattle had a little over two minutes to get another score. The team needed only about 30 seconds, though. On the fourth play of the possession, Lynch took the handoff and burst through a hole for a 24-yard touchdown run.

The score put the Seahawks up by one. They opted to go for a two-point conversion to try to go

Tight end Luke Willson (82) catches a two-point conversion to put the Seahawks up against the Packers.

up by three. But Packers defenders quickly swarmed Wilson. While running backward, the quarterback threw a desperate pass high into the air. Somehow, tight end Luke Willson was there to make the catch and give the Seahawks a 22–19 lead. The game wasn't done, though. Green Bay drove down the field and kicked a game-tying field goal with 14 seconds left to force overtime.

RUNNING FREE

The Seahawks started the extra period with the ball. They just needed a touchdown to secure the comeback. After the long completion to Baldwin, Seattle was set up in Green Bay territory. Throughout the game, Wilson had struggled to connect with Jermaine Kearse. The wide receiver had been the intended target

Receiver Jermaine Kearse (15) hangs on to the game-winning touchdown in overtime of the NFC title game.

on all four of Wilson's interceptions in the game. Kearse had yet to make a catch.

On the next play, Wilson dropped back to pass. Kearse ran down the middle of the field with a Packers defender trailing him. Wilson unleashed a 35-yard pass right into Kearse's hands. Both Kearse and the defender went tumbling into the end zone. The wide receiver was able to hold on to the ball to score the game-winning touchdown. "The will and the drive of these men is unbelievable," Wilson said after the game. "We always find a way to finish."

"WE ALWAYS FIND A WAY TO FINISH."

—RUSSELL WILSON

The Packers walked off the field stunned. The Seahawks players and coaches mobbed one another in celebration. After pulling off the 28–22 comeback win, Seattle was going back to the Super Bowl.

NFL TEAMS MAP

NFC

NFC EAST

- DALLAS COWBOYS
- NEW YORK GIANTS
- PHILADELPHIA EAGLES
- WASHINGTON COMMANDERS

NFC WEST

- ARIZONA CARDINALS
- LOS ANGELES RAMS
- SAN FRANCISCO 49ERS
- SEATTLE SEAHAWKS

NFC NORTH

- CHICAGO BEARS
- DETROIT LIONS
- GREEN BAY PACKERS
- MINNESOTA VIKINGS

NFC SOUTH

- ATLANTA FALCONS
- CAROLINA PANTHERS
- NEW ORLEANS SAINTS
- TAMPA BAY BUCCANEERS

AFC

AFC EAST

- BUFFALO BILLS
- MIAMI DOLPHINS
- NEW ENGLAND PATRIOTS
- NEW YORK JETS

AFC WEST

- DENVER BRONCOS
- KANSAS CITY CHIEFS
- LAS VEGAS RAIDERS
- LOS ANGELES CHARGERS

AFC NORTH

- BALTIMORE RAVENS
- CINCINNATI BENGALS
- CLEVELAND BROWNS
- PITTSBURGH STEELERS

AFC SOUTH

- HOUSTON TEXANS
- INDIANAPOLIS COLTS
- JACKSONVILLE JAGUARS
- TENNESSEE TITANS

Seattle is the most populous city in Washington state.

CHAPTER 2

EMERALD CITY FOOTBALL

IN 1970, THE SEATTLE METRO AREA HAD A POPULATION OF ABOUT 1.5 million people, a number that would more than double over the next 50 years. Seattle was just beginning to develop into a major city in the United States. Three years earlier, "the Emerald City" got its first major professional sports team with the arrival of basketball's SuperSonics.

The National Football League (NFL) was also growing during that time, both in popularity and in number of teams. During the 1970 season, the NFL merged with its rival league, the American Football League (AFL). In addition to gaining 10 AFL teams from the merger, the NFL also planned to expand by two teams.

Football fans in Seattle hoped their city would soon get its own team. The city began construction on a new multisport stadium in 1972

The Seahawks played in the Kingdome from 1976 to 1999.

to help attract a team. In 1974, the NFL awarded one expansion team to Tampa Bay and the second to Seattle.

The team was originally owned by the Nordstrom family, the founders of a popular department store chain that began in Seattle. By the time the NFL announced that the city was getting a team, the new stadium was halfway finished. Known as the Kingdome, the stadium featured a concrete roof that ensured fans of pro football, baseball, and basketball would never have to worry about Seattle's notorious rain.

BIRTH OF THE SEAHAWKS

Seattle's new team was set to begin play in 1976, but it first needed a nickname. In early 1975, the team ran a contest in which people could submit name ideas. The team was overwhelmed with thousands of entries, with suggestions ranging from "Aardvarks" to "Zodiacs." But "Seahawks," another name for a type of bird called an osprey, was the most popular suggestion.

For a logo, the team looked to the history of the Pacific Northwest region and the American Indian people who originally populated it. The team's hawk logo was based on the design of a mask worn by the Kwakwaka'wakw people. And the team colors of green and blue represented the colors of the environment in the region.

Wide receiver Steve Largent made seven Pro Bowls during his 14-year career with Seattle.

Seattle made a couple of key moves before the 1976 season that formed the core of the team. Quarterback Jim Zorn had joined the Dallas Cowboys in 1975 as an undrafted player, but he was released before the season started. The Seahawks picked him up in early 1976. For the next seven years, Zorn was the team's starting quarterback. He established the franchise's major career passing records, surpassing 20,000 yards and 100 touchdowns.

Wide receiver Steve Largent was an even bigger find for Seattle. The Houston Oilers were considering releasing Largent during the 1976 preseason. But the Seahawks traded Houston an eighth-round draft pick to ensure they got him. Largent became one of the greatest players in Seahawks history, setting NFL records for career catches, receiving yards, and touchdowns. He was also the first Seahawks player to be selected for the Pro Football Hall of Fame.

KNOX-ING AT THE DOOR

Fans in Seattle were excited for their new team. In 1976, the Seahawks sold 59,000 season tickets, nearly the entire capacity of the Kingdome. There was little to cheer about that first season, though. The Seahawks started 0–5 before getting their first win on the road against the Tampa Bay Buccaneers. Seattle finished with a 2–12 record, one of the worst in the league that year.

The team finally finished with its first winning season in 1978. That year, Largent recorded his first of eight seasons with more than 1,000 receiving yards. After three straight losing seasons from 1980 to 1982, the team finally saw some success in 1983 under new head coach Chuck Knox.

Chuck Knox, *center*, was the Seahawks' head coach from 1983 to 1991.

Midway through the season, Knox made a key decision by benching Zorn. The quarterback had started to show a decline in play during his eighth season with the team. Backup Dave Krieg took the place of Zorn as the starter. Krieg went 5-3 that year, throwing 18 touchdowns and helping the Seahawks to a 9-7 record. That was good enough for the team to make its first playoff appearance.

In addition to Largent, who turned in another 1,000-yard receiving season, the Seahawks leaned heavily on rookie running back Curt Warner. Seattle had selected Warner as a first-round pick in the 1983 NFL Draft. He became known for his graceful, gliding running style and his ability to rack up big numbers. Warner made the Pro Bowl in his rookie season after rushing for 1,449 yards and 13 touchdowns.

Running back Curt Warner ran for more than 1,000 yards four times with the Seahawks between 1983 and 1989.

Quarterback Dave Krieg played 12 seasons with the Seahawks.

PLAYOFF MAGIC

Seattle hosted the Denver Broncos in the first round of the playoffs in December 1983. In front of the Seahawks' home crowd, Krieg tossed three touchdowns. Seattle pulled away in the second half to win 31–7. However, Seattle faced a much tougher test the following week in the divisional round against the Miami Dolphins.

The Dolphins were the reigning conference champions, and people expected them to beat the Seahawks. To make matters worse, Seattle had a flight delay and did not arrive in Miami until 3 a.m. on the morning of the game. But the Seahawks came ready to play, and they stayed with the Dolphins throughout the back-and-forth game.

Seattle was up by four in the fourth quarter, but then Miami scored a touchdown to take a late 20–17 lead. When the Seahawks got the ball back, Krieg drove the team 66 yards in just five plays. The drive was capped with a touchdown run from Warner, his

Largent, *in blue*, hauls in a pass against the Miami Dolphins in the playoffs after the 1983 season.

second of the half. On the kickoff, Seattle forced a fumble and was set up with great field position.

A 37-yard field goal from kicker Norm Johnson gave the Seahawks 10 points in a span of 29 seconds. Kicking off again, the Seahawks forced yet another fumble. Up by seven with just over one minute remaining, the Seattle defense stopped the Miami offense to clinch the 27–20 playoff win. "Nobody thought we had a ghost of a chance of winning," said Seattle fullback Dan Doornink.

"NOBODY THOUGHT WE HAD A GHOST OF A CHANCE OF WINNING."

—DAN DOORNINK

The Seahawks' playoff run finally ended the following week. In the American Football Conference (AFC) title game, Seattle was

overwhelmed by the Los Angeles Raiders. Krieg and Zorn threw a combined five interceptions in the 30–14 loss. But with all that the Seahawks had accomplished in Knox's first season as head coach, many people felt as though bigger things were coming.

BIG HOPE FOR "THE BOZ"

The Seahawks set a team record with 12 wins in 1984 but lost a playoff rematch with the Dolphins. The team struggled the following seasons, but in 1987, Seattle picked up a player who gave fans significant hope. Linebacker Brian Bosworth had been one of the top defensive players in college football at Oklahoma. The Seahawks selected him in the 1987 supplemental draft.

Bosworth was an incredibly talented athlete, but he was also a controversial figure. Known by his nickname "the Boz," Bosworth was a confident and boastful player who often found himself in trouble both on and off the field. In college, he was suspended for using performance-enhancing drugs. But despite these issues, fans believed Bosworth could help make the Seahawks a championship contender.

Bosworth made his debut in 1987 and picked up his first career sack in his second pro game. He finished the season with four sacks, tied for third on the team. But the linebacker was probably best remembered for a *Monday Night Football* matchup between the Seahawks and the Raiders. The game was a highly anticipated meeting of two of the NFL's most promising young players in Bosworth and Raiders star running back Bo Jackson. Before the game, Bosworth vowed that he would shut Jackson down. But in the game's most memorable play,

THE 12s

The Seahawks had only been a team for eight years when they retired their first uniform number. However, the team wasn't retiring the number of a great player. In 1984, Seattle retired the number 12 to represent the fans, whose cheers are said to give the home team an extra advantage. Football fans are often referred to as "the 12th man." Today, Seahawks fans refer to themselves as "the 12s" and are considered some of the most loyal fans in the NFL. A flag bearing the number 12 is raised before every home game.

Linebacker Brian Bosworth, *left*, had two fumble recoveries during his rookie season in 1987.

Jackson ran right through Bosworth to score a touchdown. The Raiders went on to dominate the Seahawks 37–14.

After three disappointing and injury-filled years with Seattle, Bosworth retired after the 1989 season. The Seahawks had just one winning season between 1989 and 1994, although they did feature a strong defense led by tackle Cortez Kennedy. In 1992, Kennedy recorded a team-record 14 sacks and earned the NFL's Defensive Player of the Year Award. However, the Seahawks finished just 2–14 and scored the lowest number of points in the league that year. After finishing fifth in their division for the third straight time in 1994, the Seahawks had to find a way to become winners again.

Defensive tackle Cortez Kennedy made eight Pro Bowls during his 11 seasons with Seattle.

Rick Mirer was the Seahawks' main starting quarterback between 1993 and 1996.

CHAPTER 3

MAKING MOVES

While the Seahawks made efforts to improve on the field during the 1990s, they faced problems off the field. The Kingdome, which was almost 20 years old, was starting to show its age. In July 1994, just hours before a Seattle Mariners professional baseball game, four tiles fell from the stadium's roof onto the field. Nobody was hurt, but all 40,000 tiles had to be replaced for the building to be considered safe again.

The work took months. During that time, the Seahawks had to move three preseason and three regular season games to the University of Washington's Husky Stadium. Seattle couldn't play at home again until November of that year.

Team owner Ken Behring, who had purchased the Seahawks from the Nordstrom family in 1988, argued that the incident showed that the

A moving truck with Seattle's weightlifting equipment pulls into the parking lot of the old Los Angeles Rams facility in California.

Kingdome was becoming outdated and in need of replacement. Behring was willing to go extreme lengths to make his point. He believed a new stadium would never get approved in Seattle, so Behring made a surprise announcement in February 1996 that the team was moving to Anaheim, California.

Moving vans packed up the team's equipment for Southern California. The Seahawks began holding offseason practices at the old headquarters of the Rams, who had just moved from Los Angeles to St. Louis. Football fans seemed certain that the Seahawks had played their last game in Seattle.

SAVING THE SEAHAWKS

The NFL quickly stepped in. The league threatened Behring with fines of $500,000 per day until team operations returned to Seattle. King County, which operated the Kingdome, also filed lawsuits against Behring for breaking a condition from when he purchased the Seahawks that required him to keep the team in Seattle.

The NFL's intervention meant that the Seahawks were not leaving Seattle. But Behring could not continue as their owner. In 1997, the team was put up for sale with the hope that a local buyer would commit to keeping the team in the city for good.

In stepped Paul Allen. Allen was a Seattle native and co-founder of the computer company Microsoft. Allen already owned pro basketball's Portland Trail Blazers, but he was interested in buying the Seahawks if it meant helping out his hometown. "Paul was pretty open to it for one simple reason," said Seahawks radio broadcaster Steve Raible. "He believed it was good for the community."

Allen agreed to buy the team on one condition. He wanted people in the state to vote to apply $300 million of their taxpayer money toward a new Seahawks stadium. Allen said he would fund the rest. The voters approved the condition, and construction on the project began in 1998.

Paul Allen owned the Seahawks from 1997 until his death in 2018.

BUILDING ON THE FIELD

The Seahawks hired coach Mike Holmgren after the 1998 season. Holmgren was a proven winner, having won a Super Bowl with the Green Bay Packers. He was also given the title of general manager. That meant in addition to coaching, he would oversee the team's roster moves.

Mike Holmgren had an 86-74 record as the Seahawks' head coach.

Holmgren quickly built a strong team. In Holmgren's first season with the Seahawks in 1999, the team improved to 9-7, which was good enough to return to the playoffs for the first time in 11 years. Although the Seahawks lost to the Miami Dolphins in the wild-card round, the game was historic in that it was the final game in the Kingdome.

While a new stadium was being built, the Seahawks had to relocate to Husky Stadium for the 2000 and 2001 seasons. Although the team didn't make the playoffs either season, Holmgren added some important players to the roster during that time. He drafted running back Shaun Alexander and offensive lineman Steve Hutchinson. Holmgren also traded for the Packers' former backup quarterback, Matt Hasselbeck.

Offensive lineman Steve Hutchinson was inducted into the Pro Football Hall of Fame in 2020.

BUMPS ALONG THE WAY

More changes awaited Seattle

in the early 2000s. In May 2001, the NFL announced a division realignment. The Seahawks would be moving from the AFC to the NFC for the 2002 season. Also in 2002, the team finally opened its new home, which is now called Lumen Field. Despite the lack of a roof, the stadium was still loud with the cheers of passionate Seahawks fans. And fans had plenty to cheer about.

Hasselbeck turned into a Pro Bowl–level quarterback, displaying accuracy while throwing few interceptions. Alexander became one of the league's best running backs, scoring double-digit touchdowns every season from 2001 to 2005. And blocking for him were Hutchinson and offensive tackle Walter Jones, who both went on to become Hall of Famers.

In 2003, the Seahawks made it back to the playoffs after finishing the season with a 10–6 record. The team took a trip to Green Bay to play the

BLUE THUNDER

The day of a Seahawks home game is serious business around Seattle. In addition to the noise the fans generate, the stadium rumbles with the sound of "Blue Thunder." Established in 2004, Blue Thunder is the name of Seattle's drumline, which performs at home games. In a music-loving city such as Seattle, famous drummers often join the line during games. Guest drummers have included Chad Smith of the Red Hot Chili Peppers, Mike Portnoy from Dream Theater, and Matt Cameron from Seattle-based Pearl Jam.

A member of Blue Thunder plays before a Seattle home game in 2019.

Quarterback Matt Hasselbeck, *left*, prepares to pass in the wild-card round matchup between the Seahawks and Packers after the 2003 season.

Packers in the wild-card round. Seattle jumped ahead early before Green Bay took a 13–6 lead at halftime. In the third quarter, Seattle retook the lead thanks to two rushing touchdowns from Alexander. But the Packers responded with two rushing touchdowns of their own. Then with just over two minutes to play, Hasselbeck led a 67-yard drive that ended with Alexander's third touchdown of the game. That score tied the game 27–27, forcing overtime.

Seattle won the coin toss to determine who would kick and who would receive the ball to start the extra period. The referee asked Hasselbeck what the Seahawks wanted to do. "We want the ball," the quarterback said, his words broadcast to not only the TV audience but to everyone in the stadium as well. "And we're going to score."

"WE WANT THE BALL. AND WE'RE GOING TO SCORE."

—MATT HASSELBECK

Hasselbeck indeed started marching the Seahawks toward the end zone. But on the sixth play of the drive, he was intercepted by Green Bay's Al Harris. Harris ran the ball 52 yards for a touchdown to beat Seattle 33–27.

SUPER BOWL RUN

By 2005, some Seahawks fans were starting to lose patience. Holmgren had made the Seahawks competitive again, but the team had yet to win a playoff game under him. In fact, the Seahawks hadn't won a playoff game in 21 years.

But things were looking different in 2005. For the first time in franchise history, the Seahawks had an NFL Most Valuable Player (MVP) in Alexander, who led the league with 1,880 rushing yards. He also smashed the NFL record for most touchdowns in a season with 28. And the Seahawks were flying as they won a team-record 13 games.

Running back Shaun Alexander's 9,429 rushing yards and 100 rushing touchdowns are both Seattle records.

Despite the success, the Seahawks' awful playoff luck appeared as though it was going to ruin the team's magical season. In the divisional round against Washington, Alexander got hurt in the first quarter. But Hasselbeck kept the offense moving as the Seahawks snapped their playoff losing streak with a 20–10 victory.

In the NFC title game the following week, the Seahawks hosted the Carolina Panthers with a trip to the Super Bowl on the line. In front of a packed home crowd, Seattle scored first on a laser throw from Hasselbeck to tight end Jerramy Stevens. Then on the Panthers' next possession, Seattle linebacker Lofa Tatupu intercepted a pass. The Seahawks scored the first 17 points of the game, and Alexander finished the day with two rushing touchdowns. The 34–14 win sent the team to its first Super Bowl.

In Super Bowl XL, the opposing Pittsburgh Steelers were seeking their fifth title. The Seahawks had won more games than Pittsburgh

Linebacker Lofa Tatupu recorded 10 interceptions during his career with the Seahawks.

that season, but they were seen as the underdogs. Even so, many Seahawks fans took the trip to Detroit for the game hoping the predictions were wrong.

People quickly realized that the Steelers were not going to dominate. Seattle took an early lead on a field goal and gave up its first touchdown just two minutes before halftime. Although the Steelers scored on a huge 75-yard touchdown run on their second play of the third quarter, Seattle came back later in the third with a touchdown from Hasselbeck to Stevens.

The score remained 14–10 heading into the fourth quarter. Hasselbeck drove the Seahawks down to the 1-yard line with a chance to take the lead, but a holding call pushed Seattle back to the 29-yard line. Hasselbeck was sacked on the next play, and then he threw an interception. On the next drive, Pittsburgh scored to go up 21–10. That was too big a gap for the Seahawks to overcome as they suffered another heartbreaking playoff loss.

The holding call and several other controversial calls angered many Seahawks fans. After the game, Holmgren said it was as though they were playing against both the Steelers and the referees. Years later, referee Bill Leavy admitted he had made incorrect calls during the game. None of that would give the Seahawks their Super Bowl win, though. And after a 4–12 record in 2008, Holmgren left the team. But Seattle's next Super Bowl–caliber coach was just around the corner.

Hasselbeck (8) is sacked by a Pittsburgh Steelers defender during Super Bowl XL in February 2006.

Pete Carroll answers questions during a press conference introducing him as Seattle's new head coach.

CHAPTER 4

HAWKS ON TOP

AS THEY HAD WITH HIRING MIKE HOLMGREN IN 1999, THE SEAHAWKS made a big splash with their coaching hire in 2009. Pete Carroll previously coached in the NFL, but he came to Seattle after a national championship-winning career at the University of Southern California (USC). Carroll brought energy, enthusiasm, and experience to the job.

While many coaches are stoic leaders, Carroll was anything but. Carroll believed in forming close relationships with his players and understanding them as human beings, while still holding them to high standards. Players enjoyed the culture Carroll created and wanted to perform well for him.

A key personality for Carroll's Seahawks was running back Marshawn Lynch, whom the team traded for in 2010. Lynch was a powerful, bruising

Marshawn Lynch, *left*, had more than 10 rushing touchdowns in four of the seven seasons he played with Seattle.

runner, earning him the nickname "Beast Mode." Although Lynch could be one of the meanest players on the field, he was also a beloved teammate and fun-loving jokester. Lynch always let his true personality shine through, even when it led to something unusual, such as his habit of eating candy on the sideline during games. This helped cement him as a fan favorite in Seattle.

THE BEAST QUAKE

Even though the Seahawks finished 7-9 in 2010, their record was good enough to make the playoffs. However, they had to face the defending Super Bowl champion New Orleans Saints in the wild-card round. An early interception from Matt Hasselbeck helped the Saints build a quick 10–0 lead in the first quarter.

But the Seahawks refused to quit. Hasselbeck bounced back to throw four touchdown passes. Seattle had a 34–20 lead going into the fourth quarter, but the Saints cut that lead to four points with just over nine minutes to play. That was when Lynch took over the game.

Lynch dives into the end zone for a touchdown during the Seahawks' playoff game against the New Orleans Saints in January 2011.

Seattle faced second down from its own 33-yard line. Hoping to keep the clock moving, the Seahawks called a running play for Lynch. Lynch took a handoff, and after breaking through two Saints defenders, he just kept going down the field. Two more Saints got their hands on him, but Beast Mode couldn't be stopped. Another Saints defender caught up with the running back, but Lynch sent him flying with a shove of his arm. Lynch continued to leave

Safety Earl Thomas recorded 28 interceptions during his time with the Seahawks.

defenders behind him as he ran into the end zone for a 67-yard touchdown. The Seahawks held off the Saints' offense to secure a 41–36 victory.

Lynch's run became known as "the Beast Quake." The home crowd cheered so loudly that the sound was actually registered on tools used to monitor for earthquakes. Even though Seattle lost in the next round, the Beast Quake remained an iconic moment in NFL history. And the best was yet to come.

COMPLETING THE TEAM

In the 2010 draft, Carroll and general manager John Schneider began remaking the team's defense. The Seahawks selected safeties Earl Thomas and Kam Chancellor, two key pieces of the Seattle defense for most of the next decade. This was the beginning of the Seahawks' "Legion of Boom" defense, named after a group of comic book superheroes known as "the Legion of Doom."

After their breakthrough playoff win, the Seahawks continued to add to their emerging defense. In 2011, they signed cornerback Brandon Browner out of the Canadian Football League. Two other cornerbacks, Richard Sherman and Byron Maxwell, were chosen in the late rounds of the 2011 NFL Draft. These players, along with Thomas and Chancellor, formed the core of the

Legion of Boom. "Legion is like a vast army," said Chancellor. "It kind of fits the description of our unit, our brotherhood of love, trust, honesty, respect."

Although many players contributed to the Legion of Boom's success, Sherman was its vocal leader. Confident and brash, Sherman backed up his talk by being one of the best cornerbacks in NFL history. He regularly matched up with the opponent's top receiver and often shut him down.

While the Seahawks' defense was shaping up, the team still faced questions at the quarterback spot. Hasselbeck played his final season in 2010, and successor Tarvaris Jackson failed to impress. The Seahawks signed quarterback Matt Flynn ahead of the 2012 season, but rookie Russell Wilson ended up winning the

Cornerback Brandon Browner (39) returned two interceptions for touchdowns in his first season with Seattle in 2011.

starting job. Wilson, who was selected by the Seahawks in the third round of the 2012 draft, impressed coaches with his accuracy and athleticism along with his leadership.

THE TIP

Wilson proved to be the franchise quarterback that the Seahawks were looking for. Led by the young quarterback, Seattle also adopted a new look for 2012, with dark blue and neon green uniforms. By 2013, the Seahawks looked entirely different with a 13–3 record and a star quarterback in Wilson, who tossed 26 touchdowns against only nine interceptions.

While the Seahawks' offense was strong, the team was led by the Legion of Boom. The defense gave up just 231 points, the fewest in the NFL that year. The Seahawks lost just three games and by a combined total of 15 points. They steamrolled into the playoffs with high expectations.

In the divisional round, the defense did its job by shutting out the Saints through three quarters. New Orleans finally scored in the fourth, but Lynch once again came up with a big run. With 2:40 to go, the running back shoved Saints players out of the way as he

"THE FAIL MARY"

In the final seconds of a 2012 matchup against the Green Bay Packers, Seattle quarterback Russell Wilson threw a desperate pass, commonly called a Hail Mary, toward the end zone. Seahawks receiver Golden Tate struggled for the catch with Packers defender M. D. Jennings. The replay appeared to show Jennings making the interception, but Tate wrestled the ball away after the two hit the ground, so the play was deemed a touchdown. That score won Seattle the game, but the almost certainly incorrect call earned the play the nickname "the Fail Mary."

Russell Wilson, *left*, threw for 3,118 yards as a rookie.

sprinted down the sideline for a 31-yard touchdown. The score helped the Seahawks win 23–15.

With a trip to the Super Bowl on the line, the Seahawks had to face their division rival in the San Francisco 49ers in the NFC Championship Game. The 49ers also boasted a tough defense, making scoring difficult for both teams in the first half. But the Seahawks' offense picked up in the second half. Lynch ran for a 40-yard score in the third quarter, and Wilson connected with receiver Jermaine Kearse for a 35-yard touchdown in the fourth.

The Legion of Boom helped keep the Seahawks in the game. Defensive ends Michael Bennett and Cliff Avril each forced fumbles by San Francisco quarterback Colin Kaepernick in the second half.

Then in the fourth quarter, with the Seahawks holding a 20–17 lead, Chancellor intercepted Kaepernick. The Seahawks kicked a field goal to extend their lead to 23–17.

San Francisco had time for one more drive to try to win the game. Kaepernick drove the 49ers deep into Seahawks territory. With 30 seconds to go, he spotted receiver Michael Crabtree guarded one-on-one by Sherman. Kaepernick threw a deep pass into the end zone. But as the ball arrived, Sherman jumped and tipped the ball away from Crabtree. It went right into the hands of Seattle linebacker Malcolm Smith. "The Tip," as the play is known, secured the Seahawks' victory and sent them back to the Super Bowl.

Safety Kam Chancellor intercepts a pass during the NFC title game between the Seahawks and San Francisco 49ers in January 2014.

BELTING THE BRONCOS

The Seahawks faced an interesting test playing the Denver Broncos in Super Bowl XLVIII on February 2, 2014. While Seattle had allowed the fewest points during the season, Denver had scored the most

Cornerback Richard Sherman, *right*, makes "the Tip" in the NFC title game.

points in NFL history. It was a classic matchup of great offense against great defense.

On the first offensive play of the game, the Broncos' center snapped the ball over the head of star quarterback Peyton Manning. Denver recovered the ball in the end zone, which resulted in a safety and two points for the Seahawks. It only got worse for Denver from there.

Chancellor ended Denver's final possession of the first quarter with the first interception of the game. While players such as Chancellor and Sherman got most of the attention in the Legion of Boom that season, other players also played a vital role in Seattle's defense. For most of the year, Smith was not considered a star player, and he usually rotated in and out of the defense based on the situation. But in the Super Bowl, Smith had the game of his life.

Late in the second quarter, Manning was hit as he tried to throw a pass, and the ball flew up into the air and right into Smith's arms. Smith then outraced everyone to the end zone for a 69-yard touchdown to put the Seahawks ahead 22–0. The linebacker also recovered a fumble later in the game and made 10 tackles.

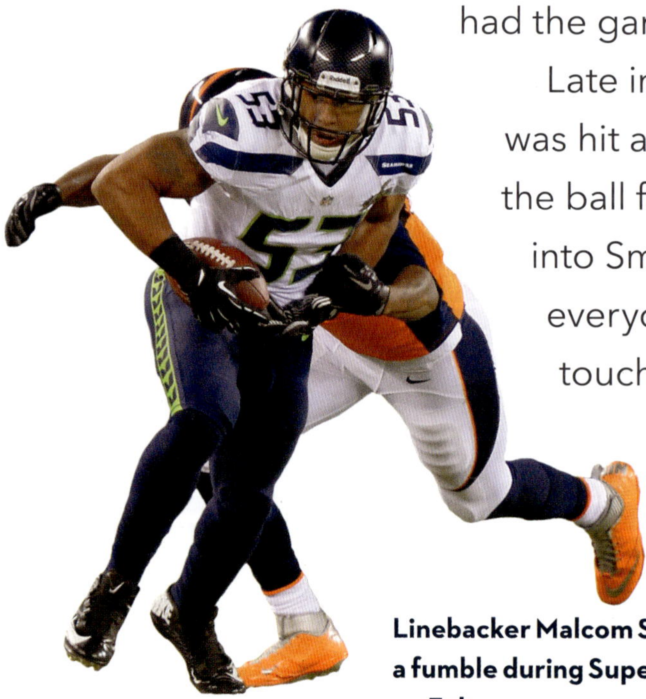

Linebacker Malcom Smith picks up a fumble during Super Bowl XLVIII on February 2, 2014.

Seattle quickly squashed any hope

Smith holds up the Vince Lombardi Trophy after the Seahawks beat the Denver Broncos in Super Bowl XLVIII.

of a Denver comeback in the second half. Seahawks wide receiver Percy Harvin returned the third-quarter kickoff 87 yards for a touchdown. Wilson added two touchdown passes on the day, and the Seattle defense held the Broncos to just one touchdown. It was an all-around team effort as the Seahawks cruised to a 43–8 victory.

For a team that had never won the Super Bowl, Seattle made it look easy. Smith was named the game's MVP, a fitting choice for a team led by its historically good defense. "To be in the Super Bowl and dominate the game says a lot about our group," said Smith.

> **"TO BE IN THE SUPER BOWL AND DOMINATE THE GAME SAYS A LOT ABOUT OUR GROUP."**
>
> **—MALCOM SMITH**

Russell Wilson made eight Pro Bowls during his 10 seasons with the Seahawks.

CHAPTER 5

AFTER THE BOOM

ALTHOUGH THE SEAHAWKS APPEARED EQUIPPED TO DEFEND THEIR SUPER Bowl title in 2014, they did not start as strongly as they had the year prior. While Seattle did win a thrilling overtime rematch against the Denver Broncos in Week 3, the team sat at 3–3 after six games. A fourth loss was looking like a possibility as the offense struggled against the Carolina Panthers in Week 8.

Seattle managed just six points and 205 yards through the first three quarters. When the Panthers took a three-point lead late in the fourth quarter, it appeared as though the game was over. But then, Russell Wilson came alive, completing all four passes he threw on an 80-yard drive, including a 23-yard touchdown to help the Seahawks win 13–9. That victory kicked off a run of nine wins in Seattle's last 10 games of the regular season. Seattle's defense gave up the fewest points in the league for the third year in a row.

The Seahawks not only made it back to the playoffs after the 2014 regular season, but they were the top seed in the conference for the second straight year. They faced the Panthers again in the divisional round. This time, there was a lot more scoring. The Seahawks held the lead for most of the game, and a 90-yard interception return from Kam Chancellor sealed the 31–17 win.

A CRUCIAL DECISION

Wilson led a thrilling comeback over the Green Bay Packers in the NFC title game. The Seahawks' overtime win sent them back to the Super Bowl. The New England Patriots awaited Seattle in Super Bowl XLIX on February 1, 2015. The matchup pitted the reigning champion against one of the greatest dynasties in sports history. It was the Legion of Boom against the Patriots' star Tom Brady, who was considered one of the greatest quarterbacks ever.

Unlike the previous year's Super Bowl, this game was close throughout. The teams traded scores to end the first half tied at 14–14. After the Seahawks kicked a field goal in the third quarter, Seattle linebacker Bobby Wagner intercepted Brady.

Kam Chancellor runs for a 90-yard interception return in the playoffs after the 2014 season.

Jermaine Kearse (15) hauls in his incredible catch during Super Bowl XLIX in February 2015.

On the next drive, Wilson hit receiver Doug Baldwin for a touchdown, giving Seattle a 24–14 lead.

However, Brady still had plenty to say as he led two touchdown drives to snatch the lead back. The second score gave New England a 28–24 lead with just over two minutes to go. That was plenty of time for Wilson, who got the Seahawks moving on their next possession with a 31-yard pass to Marshawn Lynch on first down.

Five plays later, Seattle had first down on the New England 38-yard line. Wilson dropped back and heaved a pass to Jermaine Kearse down the right sideline. Patriots cornerback Malcolm Butler reached up to knock the ball away, but Kearse kept his eyes on it. As the receiver landed on the ground, the ball bounced up off his legs. Kearse snatched it out of the air to complete an incredible 33-yard play. Then from the New England 5-yard line, Lynch muscled his way to set up Seattle at the 1-yard line.

The Seahawks just needed a touchdown to win their second straight Super Bowl title. They had Lynch, one of the most powerful runners in the game. Just about everybody expected Beast Mode to run the ball on the next play.

Instead, Wilson dropped back to pass. He quickly fired over the middle toward Baldwin, but the pass was off target. Butler intercepted the pass to end the Seahawks' drive along with their hopes of a second championship. "We played as hard as we could," Wilson said after the game. "They made one more play than we did."

The play call and its result left Seahawks fans stunned. For years, Pete Carroll's decision was questioned and debated by many people. Carroll defended the call, but it is one that Seahawks fans will likely never forget.

Wilson walks off the field after throwing an interception in Super Bowl XLIX.

THE WILSON ERA

The Super Bowl loss was a heartbreaking setback for Seattle. But with so many talented players in the prime of their careers, the Seahawks expected to stay competitive for years. A big reason was because of Wilson, who had developed into one of the best quarterbacks in the NFL. Not only was Wilson effective at running the ball and keeping plays alive, but he also delivered accurate passes, even if he didn't have the strongest arm in the league. Wilson went on to hold most of Seattle's major passing records, including career yards and touchdowns. He also set the team's single-season record for touchdown passes with 40 in 2020.

Wilson ran for 23 touchdowns during his 10-year career with Seattle.

In their quest for a third straight Super Bowl appearance, the Seahawks started slower than usual in 2015. More than halfway into the season, the team was sitting at a 4–5 record. But the Seahawks won six of their last seven games to make it to the playoffs.

In the wild-card round, Seattle had to go on the road to Minnesota to face the Vikings in one of the coldest games in NFL history. Whether it was due to the cold or great defense, both offenses struggled to get anything going. But the Seahawks broke through in the fourth quarter to score the only touchdown of the game. They then took advantage of a fumble recovery and kicked a field goal to go ahead 10–9. However, with 26 seconds left, the Vikings lined up to kick a game-winning 27-yard field goal. Instead, the ball missed wide left to give the Seahawks the win.

Seattle's offensive struggles continued into the divisional round against the Carolina Panthers. The Panthers raced out to a 31–0 lead

Chancellor, *left*, forces a fumble in the Seahawks' playoff game against the Minnesota Vikings in January 2016.

at halftime as Wilson threw two interceptions. The Seahawks did all the scoring in the second half, but they didn't have enough time to finish the comeback and lost 31–24.

MORE CHANGES

After another second-round playoff loss in 2016, the Seahawks slumped to a 9–7 record in 2017 and missed the postseason. The 2017 season was notable as the last one that the core of the Legion of Boom played together. Richard Sherman was released after the season, and Chancellor announced he would sit out 2018 before he eventually decided to retire. Other key members of the defense left over the next several years, bringing an end to one of the most dominant defenses in NFL history.

The Seahawks also suffered a more serious loss in 2018 when owner Paul Allen passed away from cancer. Allen had famously saved the team from relocating, and his period of ownership included the team's greatest seasons and its first championship. After Allen's death, control of the team passed to his sister.

Even with a depleted defense, the Seahawks made playoff runs in 2018 and 2019. The 2019 season included the return of Lynch. Lynch had retired from the Seahawks after the 2015 season. But he came back to the NFL in 2017 and played two seasons with the Oakland Raiders before returning to Seattle. In the 2019 playoffs, the Seahawks

RECORD NOISE

Since the Seahawks' stadium opened in 2002, it has been considered one of the loudest in the NFL. In a 2013 game between the Seahawks and New Orleans Saints, Seattle was recognized by Guinness World Records as having the loudest stadium in the world. The crowd noise during the game was recorded at 137.6 decibels, nearly the same volume as a jet airliner taking off. Although the record was surpassed the next year by the Kansas City Chiefs' fans, Seattle is still well known throughout the NFL as a noisy place to play.

A Seahawks fan holds up a sign during a home game in 2013.

traveled to Philadelphia and upset the Eagles 17–9. Lynch ran for a touchdown, and Wilson connected to rookie wide receiver D. K. Metcalf for a 53-yard score. However, Seattle's season ended the next week in a 28–23 loss to the Packers.

Metcalf emerged as one of the greatest receivers in Seahawks history. In 2020, he broke Steve Largent's team record for receiving yards in a season with 1,303. Despite Metcalf standing at 6 feet, 4 inches tall and weighing 235 pounds, he also had some speed.

AFTER WILSON

While the Seahawks had done a good job of staying competitive despite so many changes, they won just seven games in 2021, their

Marshawn Lynch, *center*, dives into the end zone during the playoff game between the Seahawks and Philadelphia Eagles in January 2020.

Receiver D. K. Metcalf made his first Pro Bowl after the 2020 season.

fewest wins since 2011. Wilson also dealt with a finger injury in Week 5. The veteran quarterback was one of Seattle's top success stories, but as the team declined, he was frustrated with how things were going.

The Seahawks agreed to trade Wilson to the Broncos ahead of the 2022 season. After finishing with a 9–8 record and missing the playoffs in 2023, the Seahawks took the final step in moving on from their championship years by firing Carroll. While Carroll was easily the winningest coach in team history, and his 14-year career covered some of the team's best seasons, the Seahawks had not made it past the second round of the playoffs since their loss in Super Bowl XLIX.

In 2024, the Seahawks hired new head coach Mike Macdonald. In Macdonald's first season, Seattle stayed close to the top of its division for much of the year. But in the end, the team's 10–7 record wasn't good enough to make the playoffs.

SEAHAWKS TROPHY CASE

SUPER BOWL CHAMPIONSHIPS: 1

Super Bowl XLVIII – February 2, 2014

CONFERENCE CHAMPIONSHIPS: 3

2005, 2013, 2014

DIVISION TITLES: 11

AFL West: 1988, 1999
NFC West: 2004, 2005, 2006, 2007, 2010, 2013, 2014, 2016, 2020

All stats are through the 2024 season.

Head coach Mike Macdonald high-fives a Seahawks player during the 2024 season.

Still, the always loyal Seahawks fans had hope. In 2024, talented second-year receiver Jaxon Smith-Njigba finished the season with 1,130 receiving yards and six touchdowns. On defense, young cornerback Devon Witherspoon recorded 98 tackles and was developing into one of the top players at his position. As the Seahawks looked to the future, they hoped it wouldn't be long before the crowds were once again roaring in the Pacific Northwest.

TIMELINE

1974
Seattle is awarded an expansion franchise by the NFL.

1976
The Seattle Seahawks play their inaugural NFL season, finishing 2–12.

1983
Under new head coach Chuck Knox, the Seahawks make the playoffs for the first time.

1996
Team owner Ken Behring announces Seattle's move to Anaheim, California, but the move is halted by the NFL.

1999
The Seahawks hire head coach Mike Holmgren.

2002
Seattle opens its brand-new stadium.

2006
The Seahawks play in their first Super Bowl but lose to the Pittsburgh Steelers on February 5.

2010
Seattle hires Pete Carroll as head coach.

2012
The Seahawks select Russell Wilson in the NFL Draft.

2014
On February 2, Seattle beats the Denver Broncos 43–8 to win Super Bowl XLVIII.

2015
Seattle makes its second straight Super Bowl appearance but loses to the New England Patriots on February 1.

2022
The Seahawks trade Wilson to the Broncos, ending his record-setting tenure with the team.

2024
The Seahawks hire new head coach Mike Macdonald.

GLOSSARY

draft–a system that allows teams to acquire new players coming into the league.

expansion team–a new team that is added to an existing league.

franchise–an entire sports organization.

franchise quarterback–a quarterback capable of leading a team for a number of years.

fumble–losing the ball and allowing the opponent a chance to recover it.

general manager–an executive who runs a team and is responsible for finding and signing players.

Hail Mary–a long pass that has a small chance of succeeding, usually made near the end of a game as a last-ditch effort to score.

holding–a penalty in which a player grabs another in an illegal way.

iconic–well known for excellence.

merge–join with another to create something new, such as a company, a team, or a league.

onside kick–a kickoff that is purposely short with the hope that the kicking team can recover the ball.

Pro Bowl–a postseason competition that the NFL's all-stars are invited to compete in.

professional–involving players who are paid to perform.

retire–to end one's career.

rival–an opponent with whom a player or team has a fierce and ongoing competition.

rookie–a professional athlete in his or her first year of competition.

safety–a score of two points for a team when its opponent is unable to advance the ball out of its own end zone.

supplemental draft–a special draft for players who are not eligible to be selected in the regular NFL Draft.

two-point conversion–an option for teams that have scored a touchdown to try a running or passing play from the 2-yard line for two points, instead of kicking for one point.

underdog–the person or team that is not expected to win.

veteran–someone who has played for many years.

ONLINE RESOURCES

Booklinks
NONFICTION NETWORK
FREE! ONLINE NONFICTION RESOURCES

To learn more about the Seattle Seahawks, please visit **abdobooklinks.com** or scan this QR code. These links are routinely monitored and updated to provide the most current information available.

INDEX